The Romans and Their Many Gods

Ancient Roman Mythology

Children's Greek & Roman Books

BABY PROFESSOR

EDUCATION KIDS

Speedy Publishing LLC

40 E. Main St. #1156

Newark, DE 19711

www.speedypublishing.com

Copyright 2017

In this book, we're going to cover the gods and goddesses of the Ancient Romans. So, let's get right to it!

THE RELIGION OF THE ANCIENT ROMANS

The Ancient Romans didn't believe in one god. Instead, they believed in hundreds of different gods and goddesses. The gods and goddesses each had a specific role to play.

For example, Ceres, was the goddess of a fertile harvest, so farmers would offer sacrifices and pay tribute to her if they wanted their crops to grow strong. Soldiers would offer tribute to the god of war, who was called Mars, so they would be victorious in battle.

The Romans called their huge collection of gods the Pantheon. They also named an important temple in Rome after these gods and goddesses. Most of the temples throughout the Roman Empire were built to pay tribute to only one god or goddess. They frequently had festivals and feasts to celebrate their gods.

HOW DID THE ROMANS HONOR THEIR GODS AND GODDESSES?

The Romans believed that terrible things would happen if they didn't keep their gods happy. To keep them happy, they worshipped them and prayed to them by offering sacrifices of animals, such as sheep, pigs, and bulls. Horses that won important chariot races were sacrificed as well.

They believed that each god preferred to have a specific type of animal for his sacrifice. The more powerful the god was, the more elaborate the sacrifice would need to be. The Romans also offered precious objects such as jewels and sometimes they also offered foods, such as milk, wine, and cheese.

There were elaborate rituals associated with sacrificing animals and the priests in the temple would cut up the animals in a specific way to make sure the animal was worthy to be used as a sacrifice. The organs of the animal would be burned at the altar as part of the ritual.

If anything went wrong during the ritual, it would have to be performed over again so the gods would not be angry!

WHERE DID THE ROMAN GODS COME FROM?

Before Rome was a huge city, the surrounding lands around it were called Latium. The Latin villagers who lived there were very superstitious. They believed not only in hundreds of gods but also in spirits.

At the beginning, the Romans thought of their gods as faceless spirits. They were powerful but they didn't look like humans or animals. However, as the Roman Empire grew and became more powerful, they were introduced to Greek and Etruscan cultures.

At that time, the Greeks were the dominant civilization in the area. The Greeks had a very elaborate collection of their own gods and their gods looked like humans, but they were much more powerful than humans.

When the Romans conquered the Greeks in 146 BC, they brought much of Greek culture into their lives and adapted it to suit their purposes. They did the same thing with the Greek gods and goddesses.

Sometimes the Latin god and a god from the Greek religion were very similar so they were adapted the two into one. For example, the old Latin god for fire was Vulcan. The Greeks had a god who was a blacksmith. His name was Hephaestus. So, the Romans merged the two gods together. This "new" god was called Vulcan but was pictured as a blacksmith.

HE MAJOR ROMAN GODS AND GODDESSES

Although there were hundreds of gods and goddesses, there were a major group of 12 that the Romans called the Dii Consentes. In this group there were 6 gods and 6 goddesses.

The gods were:

- Jupiter, known as Zeus by the Greeks
- Mars, known as Ares by the Greeks
- Neptune, known as Poseidon by the Greeks
- Apollo, also known as Apollo by the Greeks
- Mercury, known as Hermes by the Greeks
- Vulcan, known as Hephaestus by the Greeks

The goddesses were:

- Juno, known as Hera by the Greeks
- Venus, known as Aphrodite by the Greeks
- Minerva, known as Athena by the Greeks
- Diana, known as Artemis by the Greeks
- Ceres, known as Demeter by the Greeks
- Venus, known as Aphrodite by the Greeks
- Vesta, known as Hestia by the Greeks

HEKATE

DETAILS ABOUT THE DII CONSENTES

It will help you remember the names of the gods and goddesses, if you think of them as male and female couples. Some were couples like a married couple and others were not. Sometimes they were just paired together in famous stories, which we call myths today.

For example, Jupiter and his wife Juno were a married couple. Apollo and Diana were a pair because they were twins. The other pairs were Mars and Venus, Neptune and Minerva, Mercury and Ceres, and Vulcan and Vesta.

JUPITER

Although the gods and goddesses were very powerful, some had more power than others. Jupiter was the most powerful of the gods. He was the main god of the Ancient Romans. He's often pictured as holding thunderbolts in his hands. He could throw these thunderbolts down upon the Earth when he was angry. He was also considered to be the god of the heavens and sky. His role included enforcement of human laws as well. He made his desires known through the use of an oracle, a priest or priestess who interpreted the communication from the gods. The largest temple in the city of Rome was the temple built in honor of Jupiter located on Capitoline Hill.

JUNO

Juno was Jupiter's wife as well as his sister. She was considered to be the protector of Rome. She was also worshipped as the goddess of all women and as such she was the goddess of fertility. The upper classes of Rome worshipped her, Jupiter, and Minerva as part of a group of three divine beings. She was frequently depicted with peacocks and pomegranates to symbolize her as a fertile queen.

MARS

With the exception of Jupiter, Mars was the most aggressive and strongest of the gods. He was also the most feared since he was considered to be the god of war. He is usually pictured as armed for battle. Mars, the red planet, is named after him.

VENUS

Venus was the most beautiful of all the goddesses. She represented love, female charm, and breathtaking beauty. She was born out of the foam from the sea and she is frequently pictured as standing or sitting on a seashell as she rises from the waters. In some mythological stories, Venus and Mars have a son named Cupid.

NEPTUNE

Neptune was the forceful god of the waters. Sailors would worship Neptune and ask for his favor before they set out to travel over stormy seas. He is frequently pictured with a fishing spear that has three prongs called a trident.

MINERVA

Neptune and Jupiter were brothers so Minerva was Neptune's niece. She had no mother but came into being simply from Jupiter's mind. She's considered to be the goddess of wisdom and knowledge. She's also the goddess of crafts and medicine. Her symbol is the owl and this is probably where the idea of owls being wise originated.

APOLLO

Apollo was the handsome, young, athletic god of the sun. He was influential in everyday justice and helped to promote tolerance among the different social classes. He was well-liked among the other gods and goddesses. Apollo and Diana are considered to be a pair because they were twin brother and sister.

DIANA

Diana was the goddess of the woods and hunting. She's frequently pictured with her hunting arrows and it was thought that she had the power to speak to and control animals. She was also the goddess of the moon and childbirth, although she never had any children herself.

MERCURY

Mercury was the god of profitable trade. Merchants would worship him so they could sell their wares. Mercury was frequently pictured with winged feet as well as a staff with two snakes.

CERES

Frequently shown carrying a huge bundle of grain, Ceres is the goddess of an abundant harvest. She was also thought of as the goddess who brought the change in season.

VULCAN

Vulcan was the god of the underworld. When he was angry or provoked, out-of-control fires and volcanoes would erupt. He was depicted as a blacksmith and sometimes shown creating armor for both gods and heroes.

VESTA

Vesta and Vulcan are associated as a pair because Vesta is connected to fire as well. Instead of aggressive fire, she represents the fire that keeps a home warm as well as the type of fire that is burned in a sacred temple.

CHRISTIANITY COMES TO ROME

In 312 AD, the emperor of Rome, Constantine the Great, was about to go into battle. The night before his battle he had a dream where Christ spoke to him. He won the battle and converted the entire Roman Empire to Christianity. From then forward, the Roman Empire had Christian beliefs.

Awesome! Now you know more about the gods and goddesses of Ancient Rome. You can find more books about Ancient Rome and Ancient Greece from Baby Professor by searching the website of your favorite book retailer.